Afterlife

Barbara Hole

Poems by
George T. Hole

Buffalo Arts Publishing

Afterlife. Copyright © 2025 by George T. Hole. Printed in the United States of America. All rights reserved. No part of this book may be reproduced or transmitted in any form or by any means without written permission of the author. For information, address Buffalo Arts Publishing, 179 Greenfield Drive, Tonawanda, NY 14150

Email: info@buffaloartspublishing.com

Cover design by Len Kagelmacher

ISBN 978-1-950006-29-8

For Barbara Hole

7.15.1946–8.25.2023

Poems

Gravity

Too late to pray

We used to say

Leave the examination room

What

Afterlife

Can't say

If not grief

Confess

If we had more time

An extra toothbrush

Reaching to hold your hand

It's time

Come home

They say life

Gravity

Einstein realized
In a gravitational field
        a man falling

The doctor said she would
Live to 100 like her mother
        a man falling does

She was having difficulty
Swallowing solid food
        a man falling does not

Pancreatic cancer
Prognosis: 6 months
        a man falling does not feel

6 months 4 days later
His own weight, in grief
        a man falling does not feel

Too late to pray

Not asking the Red Sea to open
or Jesus to come back from the dead
so I might believe in an afterlife.

Not wishing a replay
of Lazarus, lucky guy,
coming back from the dead.

Not praying for the dying
except now, holding on, vexed,
for her, lying cradled next to me,

Now a banquet table for cancer.
Hear me! Heaven. Wake up.
She needs your miracle angel. Now.

We used to say *I love you*

Mornings I squeeze orange and lemon
in one of your ugly souvenir mugs
add honey and hot water. Stir.
Climb the stairs—Christ not yet-
Can't let this be the last time.

I set it down bedside. If awake,
you lip-sync *Thank you,* (a wisp
of gratitude) seems all you can say.
Or you refuse to wake,
wake up to your life, what's left.

Seems like this life belongs
to someone else whose cells
multiply faster than loaves
gone stale and fishes, like hope,
gone to rot, by what the doctor

said matter-of-factly,
Put your affairs in order.
Said more, *There is no cure*.
What did we used to say?
Used to be?

Leave the exam room

Go back through the waiting room.
Hold on to the air.
Hide your wobble
from those with forearm wrapped
with orange gauze,
hiding the blood draw and anxiety
about being called next.

Know the sign:
Place Hand Here
to open the automatic door.
Forget the curse: *No Cure*.
Practice gratitude.
Wish for a pardon.
Crave sleep. Not your final one.

Use subtraction
to count your future.
Pray for a miracle. Or an afterlife.
Smile, your family and doctor
are huddling, their desperate faces,
looking away, are as lonely
as is your own.

What

What difference would it have made if
She had closed her mouth herself
—not that she had anything left unsaid.

But that gaping hole in her cancer shrunken face
Was an insult to beauty itself, and a warning
A vengeful cyclops was taking its measure of me.

Was she at peace when the nurse closed her eyes,
Dead, and against my request told me
She could not close my wife's gaping mouth?

Held back, a fist-full rage against the nurse,
No, against this spoiled beauty, no
Against the self that wanted lip to lip, yes,

Tongue to tongue, just one more kiss, whatever
The bitter consequences. I must not to be
Left with this gruesome last memory.

Afterlife

You said
The minister's answer
Was reassuring.

You didn't want to hear
What I had to say.
So, if somehow you got there,
Surprise me, what's it like?

I need to tell you
I took off my wedding ring.
It's about time.

Close to the end,
When you said you couldn't sleep
I rolled over, away from facing you.
You never complained.

The bedroom clock light,
I explained, kept me awake.
Since then, I unplugged it.

You can't say anymore
That I steal all the blankets.
I sleep only on my side of the bed now.
I don't wrinkle the sheets on yours.

I'm telling only you
I put my wedding ring
In the container under the bed
Holding your ashes.
Your ring was cremated with you.

Can't say

She fought it
it's a cliché, hearsay.

not like an accident
broken glass, bumper on the curb

yellow ribbon of police tape
the tow truck

not like the body
is around somewhere

went up in smoke
not like the furnace at the steel mill

no singing
over the rainbow

like nothing else
no sunset, sunrise

a black hole
can't say

If not grief

Listen to the eulogy for you.
Free a tear or make-believe there is one.

Your death is not a cosmic crime. "Lost love;
Last love" is not a battle cry.

The minister's sermon strikes a few feeble sparks.
Whimper to myself: Organ too loud. Pew hard.

Share the sign of peace. Shake hands.
Others loved her too.

Stand with the congregation. Sing.
At least make your mouth move.

Mumble "forgive us our trespasses."
Feel a guilt-string plucked. Then cut.

Cut down. Like the flowers
Decorating the alter. Quick to wilt.

What terror
If grief refuses to heal?

Broken heart, break, as light breaks
Passing through the stained-glass windows.

Oh, broken heart,
Break open.

An extra tooth brush

Sheets. Twisted up in them.
Pillow must have fallen to the floor.

I reached for your hand.
The hollow in our mattress bears your imprint.

Mornings you used to tell me your dreams.
And ask what they meant.

I'm having the same dream. Are you safe?
The grandkids ask *Where's Baba?*

They play with the old dial phone. Geo asked
How do dead people get to heaven?

Your *Book of Prayers* is still open on your nightstand.
God did not bargain.

Our daughters have emptied your closet.
All your clothes have gone to the *Good Will*

I can't believe how many eye-glasses and cases I found.
You did love multiples of things.

Remember when we travelled?
You always took an extra tooth brush.

And extra other stuff.
For just-in-case.

It has gone beyond just-in-case.
Give back an extra one of you.

What if

We had more time
Would we be different?
Not the same old: *What do you want
For dinner?* Not the same weather
With more climate change mixed in.

Why did you want to watch
The news night after night?
Nothing hopeful. Followed by *Jeopardy*.
Neither of us knew any answers.
Or are quick enough.

In the dark the numerals
On the alarm clock lit up red.
You said you can't sleep.
I rolled over on my side.
I could have held you instead.

I leaned close to whisper to Margaret
At her wake a message for you:
I took off my wedding ring.
Put it in the jar holding your ashes.
Your ring was cremated with you.

Confess

Confess, I heard the minister say.
Our love is fickle.
Our harmful ways hurt others.
In silence the congregation confesses.
Resolves to change.

In your church I twist
My wedding ring around my finger.
Confess. As if you could hear me,
Your ring was not cremated.
It's not in your ashes under the bed.

Yes,
Your side of our bed is empty,
Next to
An emptiness
On mine.

Reaching to hold your hand

Your memorial service ended, everyone said, joyfully.
Church was full. Choir sang the music you chose.
A solemn beauty filled the emptiness.
Listening to eulogies by Ann and Liz
You would have laughed and cried. As we did.
And prayed the promise for your afterlife.

Kids and I wore one of your silk scarfs.
As you might have guessed, Lauren
Tied mine on in one of your stylish ways.
At the reception people mingled until quite late.
Favorite stories. Somber moments. Finally,
Time to change into my pajamas and slippers.

On the nightstand, on your side of the bed,
I catch a glanced of our photograph. You know,
The one of us at Liz's wedding.
Why do you give me that look now?
Don't ask me to remember the names
Of all who offered condolences. And those absent.

I set a glass of Tanqueray on your dressing table,
As we did when we dressed to go out.
You never finished yours.
Put it in a plastic cup. Drank as I drove.
Remember, you imagined the scene of being arrested,
For being an intoxicated back-seat driver.

Oh, this day aching, adrift, numb.
Ice in your glass has melted.
I finish your gin. Feel drunk.
Too late to ask, but why
With dire warning signs, in spite of,
Did you refused pleas to go to the doctor?

Time for sleep. To reaching out
To hold your hand
Then say, in our dark bed,
As I always did, *Sweet dreams.*
Just so you know,
I'm god-damn mad.

It's time

Ecclesiastes never said *it's time*
To take off your wedding ring.

One body is still alive.
The other ashes.

Use Vaseline. It's hard to
Twist it over my knuckle.

Read the inside inscription.
Need a magnifying glass.

Between two sets of initials intact,
A date.

Put it in my unused hearing-aid case.
Put hers in too.

My thumb, being faithful, feels
For the missing ring. Feels for her.

If someone spreads my ashes
Will any particle find hers?

Come home

Left New Year's Eve celebration early.
Can't sing old acquaintances be forgotten.

Can't kiss you at midnight. Ever again.
I came home.

Closed the garage door.
Walked back up the icy driveway.

Damned the crows for roosting
In my endangered elm tree

Yelled. Yelled louder. Their
Wings slapped the air

As an out-of-tune choir of complaints.
They will be back.

I unlocked the front door. Told myself
Go straight to bed.

Don't fall asleep
As a miner, underground,

As his head lamp flickered out.
Don't disappear

In what little survives,
Your ashes, still warm.

They say

life will begin again
I half awoke, alarmed after
dreaming of you.
oh god yes.

recite: *be careful.*
hold on both railings
going down the stairs.
in the dark.

feed the dogs. read the news.
pour more coffee. who's that
unshaven face in a steamed mirror?
make a sour face. scare it away.

dare. do not put on a public face
to assure all your friends
I am fine. my mantra cover-up.
I whimper inside.

refuse to be an empty voice
praying beside an empty bed
my soul to take,
cry out. *feel.*

feel even the thick
choking they call grief.
feel inside loss.
I can't say.

www.ingramcontent.com/pod-product-compliance
Lightning Source LLC
Chambersburg PA
CBHW061811070526
44586CB00024B/2807